Worlds Of Imagination

Edited By Megan Roberts

First published in Great Britain in 2019 by:

Young Writers
Remus House
Coltsfoot Drive
Peterborough
PE2 9BF
Telephone: 01733 890066
Website: www.youngwriters.co.uk

FOREWORD

Here at Young Writers, we love to let imaginations run wild and creativity go crazy. Our aim is to encourage young people to get their creative juices flowing and put pen to paper. Each competition is tailored to the relevant age group, hopefully giving each pupil the inspiration and incentive to create their own piece of creative writing, whether it's a poem or a short story. By allowing them to see their own work in print, we know their confidence and love for the written word will grow.

For our latest competition Poetry Wonderland, we invited primary school pupils to create wild and wonderful poems on any topic they liked – the only limits were the limits of their imagination! Using poetry as their magic wand, these young poets have conjured up worlds, creatures and situations that will amaze and astound or scare and startle! Using a variety of poetic forms of their own choosing, they have allowed us to get a glimpse into their vivid imaginations. We hope you enjoy wandering through the wonders of this book as much as we have.

CONTENTS

Preston Harrowing (10)	60
Evie Lester (11)	61
Derrick Bowditch (10)	62

Mendham Primary School, Mendham

Emily D (9)	63
Georgia Hearney (8)	64
Rishi French (8)	66
Tess Walker (9)	67
Emily (7)	68
Aidan Layton Scott (9)	69
Barney (7)	70
Luca Lambourn-Brown (8)	71
Harry Mattocks (7)	72
Ellie Brown (8)	73
James (7)	74
Jackson R (7)	75

Mill Hill Primary School, Sunderland

Lily Mersh (9)	76
Ava Mae Swinburne (8)	79
Toni Padgett (9)	80
Grace Wheeler (9)	82
Eden-Lilly Isaacson (8)	84
Chloe Duncton (8)	85
Sarah Grace Ivy Lovstad (9)	86
Maisie Wilson (8)	87
Oscar Drew (8)	88
Raef Clegg-Cawood (9)	89
Heidi Pantall (9)	90
Chloe Hill (9)	91
Warren Dean Edwards (8)	92
Megan O'Brien (9)	93

Northfield St Nicholas Primary School, Lowestoft

Lexi Tindsley (10)	94
Kaitlin Grace Cadence Collis (9)	95
Evie Armitage (7)	96

Megan-Jane Davey (8)	97

Salisbury Primary School, Manor Park

Mia Iman Akinola (10)	98
Simrah Rahman (9)	99
Shaurya Umesh (9)	100
Shaeba Hossain (9)	102
Hamza Abad (9)	103
Elizabeth-Rose Kelly (9)	104

South Lee School, Bury St Edmunds

Islay de Gonville Bromhead (7)	105
Charlotte Grigg (7)	106
Daisy Katherine Martineau (7)	107
Darcey O'Farrell (7)	108
Amélie Grace Swanton (7)	109
Alev Warwick (8)	110
Sophie Johnson (7)	111
Elli O'Dwyer (8)	112

Stalham Academy, Stalham

Beth Patterson (9)	113
Phoebe Laws (9)	114
Olivia Ford (8)	115
Kaitlin Collins (10)	116
Zebedee Mixer (9)	117
Phoebe Sue Dorrington (7)	118
Amy Frisby (11)	119
Ben Townshend (7)	120

Tregadillett Primary School, Tregadillett

Tegan Barrett (11)	121
Ebony Seedell (9)	122
Ava-Grace Phoebe Barrett (9)	124
Leah Trewin (11)	125

Uplands Primary School, Sandhurst

Freya Mepham-Gilbert (7)	126
Payton Rae De Villiers (8)	127
Mariam Jabang (7)	128

Weeting (VC) Primary School, Weeting

Ruby Violet Follen (10)	129
Eloise Grass (9)	130
Dorothy Childerhouse (9)	131
Sienna Lilly Lexi White (10)	132
Ellie Doll Ellis (8)	133
Sophia Rose Harrison (9)	134

Woodbridge Primary School, Woodbridge

Lou Lou Rolfe (9)	135
Andrew Hunter Huisman (9)	136
Cate Hesketh (8)	137
Matilda Wade (9)	138
Maggie Vinton (8)	139

The Poems

Miss Trunchbull

Miss Trunchbull is an evil lady
She is definitely quite crazy
She is terribly tall
Makes children feel small
Her expression is a bit shady

She shows a lot of aggression
To pupils to make a confession
She goes hokey pokey
Into the chokey
It's enough to give you depression!

Miss Trunchbull is a filthy creature
She is also a terrible teacher
She wears bossy boots
She wears smoky suits
What a horrible creature-teacher!

Cian Smailes (8)
Cromwell Academy, Hinchingbrooke Park

Miss Honey

A young teacher known as Jennifer
Her full name is Miss Jennifer Honey
She was so clever like a little honey bee
She was always dreaming of a beautiful sea
She always had enough money
She always smelt like a beautiful pot of honey
She taught children at school for free

Miss Honey had such a clever mind
She was also very kind
She had a lot of money
She was so cute, like a bunny
She always had a special secret bind.

Sandra Orligora (9)
Cromwell Academy, Hinchingbrooke Park

Miss Trunchbull

Miss Trunchbull is very tall
She makes everybody else look small
She puts people in the chokey
And it gets very smoky
She is really despised by all

Miss Trunchbull is a fiery one
She really isn't much fun
Everyone hates the school
Because she is so cruel
If you see her, you'd better run.

Ernie Hill (9)
Cromwell Academy, Hinchingbrooke Park

Miss Honey

A kind teacher known as Miss Honey
When working at school, was so sunny
She started to dream
That she'd be on a team
That would be so very funny

She was lovely to everyone she met
Kind, lovely, caring and yet
If you were unkind
She would still always find
A reason to still like you, I bet.

Tia Jackson (9)
Cromwell Academy, Hinchingbrooke Park

Miss Honey

A young teacher known as Miss Honey
Was so awfully funny
She laughed and joked
Until everyone choked
Sadly, she didn't have much money

Miss Honey was an amazing teacher
Unlike Miss Trunchbull, a horrible creature
She's really nice
She's got some spice
She has a nice feature.

Alexander Tulip (8)
Cromwell Academy, Hinchingbrooke Park

Mr Wormwood

Mr Wormwood was a complete idiot
He was always extremely hideous
He clearly had no brains
No smartness remains
How selfish he was, was infinite

Mr Wormwood was very boastful
Not at all hopeful
At work, he would cheat
'Til he came to a defeat
Wormwood was never really social.

Beatrix Weston (9)
Cromwell Academy, Hinchingbrooke Park

Miss Honey

All children love Miss Honey
She is just as soft as a bunny
All through the day
Come what may
Her nature is always sunny

Miss Trunchbull hates her
But she is the children's favourite professor
Miss Honey is so giving
She is always loving
Miss Honey is so clever.

Madeleine White (9)
Cromwell Academy, Hinchingbrooke Park

Matilda

Matilda was very clever
She could even write with a feather
She was as bright as a star
She would always go far

She was not made of money
But was very bright and sunny
She read lots of books
Didn't care about looks
And loved her teacher, Miss Honey!

Lucas Hull (9)
Cromwell Academy, Hinchingbrooke Park

Miss Trunchbull

Miss Trunchbull was a complete nightmare
She shouted everywhere
She called the children weak
And wouldn't let them speak
Which I don't think was fair.

Lydia Spencer (8)
Cromwell Academy, Hinchingbrooke Park

Matilda

There once was a girl called Matilda
Who could never be any weirder
So she started being clever
Not like her stupid, old father
Who painted his hair silver.

Emilia Lambert (9)
Cromwell Academy, Hinchingbrooke Park

Miss Trunchbull

Everyone dislikes Miss Trunchbull
She makes everyone look small
She is always aggressive
She makes the world depressive
She is really hated by all.

Kyla O'Connor (9)
Cromwell Academy, Hinchingbrooke Park

Miss Honey

A kind teacher known as Miss Honey
Was gentle, helpful and funny
She was always brave
To her class, she gave her time
And she was always sunny.

Stefan Labanowski (8)
Cromwell Academy, Hinchingbrooke Park

Miss Honey

A young teacher known as Miss Honey
She was always very funny
She laughed and joked
Until they nearly choked
She started to feel rather sunny!

Zsofi Lambert (9)

Cromwell Academy, Hinchingbrooke Park

The Wacky World

What a wonderful world that we can see
Planets talking like it's as normal as it can be
If you didn't see, I bet you wouldn't believe me
The sweet smell of the delicious caramel falls
And the jumping, fluffy rabbits bouncing on their paws
The UFO lollies, sweet like a jar full of honey
Honey smells so wonderful and is so runny
The mushrooms look normal
Oh, wait, they don't. They disappear with a touch
So really, you don't see them very much

Under your feet, pink is the colour you see
Grass doesn't exist obviously

However, you can't not like this wacky world
It's so wonderfully weird
Green goo instead of rain
Mythical creatures everywhere you look
Don't you just love the imagination?

Amelia Clements (11)
Gunton Primary Academy, Lowestoft

Pigeon On The Underground

Today, I took a trip on the Underground
and got to see the sights.
On my way, I found some chocolate doughnuts
and other tasty bites.
My first stop was Big Ben, and then, Madame Tussaud's,
I travelled then to Waterloo and saw the House of Lords.
I flew then for a very long time, and from the corner of my eye
Was something very big and round, it was called the London Eye
I thought, *what I fancy next is a lovely cup of tea*
So I got on the train to Buckingham Palace
and had afternoon tea with the Queen.
I felt very tired now and I could feel some rain,
so I flew back to Euston Station
and got on the fastest train.

Ella Mae Westgate (8)

Gunton Primary Academy, Lowestoft

Dragon In My Pocket

I have a little secret
Not even my best friend knows
It goes everywhere with me
In the day, it even glows

I have a little secret
It helps me when I'm stuck
Especially with calculating
It always brings me luck

I have a little secret
It keeps me warm at night
And also helps me eat my greens
When I can't take another bite

I have a little secret
It always makes me laugh
Even when I'm feeling down
It keeps me on the right path

I have a little secret
I don't know where I'd be

Without my lovely and fluffy friend
There would be no dragon and me.

Sofia Rose Smith (9)
Gunton Primary Academy, Lowestoft

Today At School I Learnt

Today at school, I learnt...
Today at school, I learnt...
Wait, I can't remember
Don't tell anyone

Okay, day two and, today, I can remember
We added and subtracted numerous numbers
Then, what did we do?
Wait for day three and I'll tell you!

It's day three and, today, I learnt how to fly
I flew as high as the sky
Finally and most importantly
I won't talk about that because it was extremely tragic

Finally, it's the last day of my term
Sadly, I still have to learn
That's including the boring, old theme
If it's too hard, I'll be blowing off steam.

Phoebe Pierpoint (9)
Gunton Primary Academy, Lowestoft

Just Imagine If

Just imagine if you woke up this morning
To find your house was made out of sweets
And every single room
Was filled with delightful treats!

Just imagine if you went to a planet
With a cupcake in the middle
And a cherry on the top
It was gone in the blink of an eye
I wonder where it went!

Just imagine if you had a dragon as a pet
And you called it Giggles
It fed on chocolate and the world!

Just imagine if your favourite story came to life
The characters became your friends
And made all the decisions
How would you send them back?

Izzy Reeve (9)
Gunton Primary Academy, Lowestoft

Above The Clouds Of Wonderland!

Sitting on cotton candy clouds
Watching the sun rise from the east
Running as fast as I could
To get to the fizzy strips of colour
Climbing up the rainbow
I got to the top!
Looking at the breathtaking scenery
I hear the unicorns munching on lollipops!
After my delicious strawberry lace lollipop
I climbed down the rainbow, feeling a bit peckish
I ate a piece of the rainbow and chocolate grass!
Spotting my pet dragon
Running over to him
Giving him a colossal hug
We ran around the place
Until we were so tired
It was the best sleep ever!

Evie Smith (9)
Gunton Primary Academy, Lowestoft

The Mole And The Hole

There was a mole
Who dug a hole
On a bowling green.
He watched the scores on a great big screen.

The bowlers came out to play,
Saw the molehill and said, "No way!"
Out popped the mole's head
And said, "I'm Fred!"

The bowler said, "Fred must leave!
A mole and a bowler is too much of a squeeze."
Fred said, "With my holes
This green will be more able,
So you could use it as a snooker table."

So, the bowlers said, "Goodbye!"
And Fred said, "Must fly!"

Max Thomas Denny (8)
Gunton Primary Academy, Lowestoft

A Bunny With Money

I had a little Bunny who took all of my money.
I said, "Look here Bunny, you're just not funny."
He had a cheeky grin, I thought I would win
But I landed on the floor as he ran out the door
With a *hop, hop, hop.*

As time went past, I thought the money wouldn't last.
Then, one day, post came my way.
Postcards from the Bunny who looked very sunny
Dancing in Ibiza, eating a pizza,
In St Helen's eating watermelons,
Doing a dance in France
With a *hop, hop, hop.*

Theo William-Harvey Stimson (8)
Gunton Primary Academy, Lowestoft

Food Wonderland

I love French toast
But snails are gross
I eat it all day
I eat it all night
The baguette shines bright
Flaky croissant for breakfast
It'll disappear pretty fast

In Food Wonderland

I love it here in Candyland
They even have a sugar band
I don't know what I love more
The candy castle or my chocolate drawer
In the middle of the land, there is a liquorice slide
It's such an amazing ride

In Food Wonderland.

Ella Ivory (10) & Ruby Ann Shelley Wisher
Gunton Primary Academy, Lowestoft

Wonderful Stars

Up in space, you can see so many stars
There are so many stars
You can't even count them all
I just wonder how many there are
But, you can only see the stars at night
As it's night-time, I should be going to sleep
With the moon so big
As I'm going to sleep
I'm still wondering
How many stars are up in space...

Sean Vale (8)
Gunton Primary Academy, Lowestoft

The Joys Of Football

F ootball is the best sport ever

O MG! What a save from Alisson

O wen scores another goal for Liverpool - the good times

T o be part of a team is just fantastic

B rilliant in fact!

A bsolutely, always

L aughing and joking and

L ots of love goes to Liverpool - my favourite team.

Jack Trowbridge (10)
Gunton Primary Academy, Lowestoft

Hospitals

H ospitals are places that
O versee people who are
S icker than me
P aramedics put on the sirens
I n a rush, in a flash.
T reating people after a crash
A mbulances, stretchers and X-ray machines.
L ives lived successfully
S aved by the hospital heroes.

George Trowbridge (8)
Gunton Primary Academy, Lowestoft

Alien Came For Tea!

An alien came down
He came to my town
I invited him for tea
He sat down next to me
We devoured our moon rocks
But, oh my gosh, it smelled like
My dad's smelly socks
After tea, we went to play
Okay, I wished he could stay
He had to go back to the moon
I hoped to see him soon.

Dylan White (10)
Gunton Primary Academy, Lowestoft

My Secret Pet

I have a secret pet
Who lives in my pocket
He came from up above
And flew down in a rocket
He has long, pink fur
And a green, twisty tail
He gives off a purr
When I tell him a tale
I have a secret pet
Who lives in my pocket
He told me one day
We will fly in a rocket.

Willow Bleu Daniels-Sutton (8)
Gunton Primary Academy, Lowestoft

I See Unicorns

Unicorns are all sorts such as:
Desert flames, light sandy-brown.
Shadow nights, dark as night.
Water moons, white like the first fall of snow.
Ice wanderers, pale cream.
Woodland flowers, covered in different petals.
Storm chasers, different colours.
Mountain jewels, dove grey.

Hannah Godbold (10)

Gunton Primary Academy, Lowestoft

Puppies

P uppies are adorable
U nbelievably cute
P uppies like to play
P uppies are furry
I would love to have one
E very single one is enthusiastic
S o everyone is happy, it will always be in their hearts.

Ellie Rutter (9)
Gunton Primary Academy, Lowestoft

Life Is Different

Different life, it's all upside-down.
Running on the ceiling, not on the floor.
Jumping on your head, not on your feet.
Sleeping on the stars, not in bed.
Driving on the clouds, not on the road.
Life is different, but it's good.

Ruby Simpson (9)
Gunton Primary Academy, Lowestoft

Lucy And Santa Have A Picnic

I teleported with Lucy to Sweetland
Where trees were made of lollipops
Roads were made of chocolate
There was even a chocolate fountain
Lucy was amazed
We rode an amazing chocolate roller coaster
All the way to the sun
The birds up high were tweeting a happy song
But, the magic candy cane ran out
It was time to leave, but Lucy didn't want to go
"Please can we stay forever?"
"I'm afraid the answer is no."

William Calcutt (7)
Hadrian Primary School, South Shields

A Rainbow Day

There was something that I'd never tasted before
A rainbow milkshake
It tasted like a unicorn
Doors that tasted like marshmallows
There were houses with wings
A unicorn with a yellow horn
I saw a rainbow milkshake ocean
There, on the ground
Was a pink and blue sapphire
But, a pink, blonde fairy ran out of the sky
The ground was light pink
I also noticed the glittery sky
If you don't believe, dream it.

Rabiya Malik (7)
Hadrian Primary School, South Shields

Learning To Fly

I learned to fly
I don't know why
It's just that some dragons came out of the sky
They taught me how to fly
I flew up to a cloud that was shouting out loud
The closer I came, the more I rowed
I knew it was ridiculous, a cloud
That could shout out loud
But this was Imagination Land
Where you could be in a big brass band
The place where your dreams come true
You just have to believe in you.

Lola Zoe Foden (7)
Hadrian Primary School, South Shields

Cars On Ice

My plan didn't go as planned
The cars slipped, slid all over the place
All the cars were crashing into each other
The cars slipped from side to side, it was rickety
After a moment, I smelled the clutch
It smelled like jam
Oh no! I need petrol! I slowly stopped
I filled my car with bubblegum
I got out of my car
Loads of cars came at me
I didn't get it, it was just my imagination.

Oscar Thacker (7)
Hadrian Primary School, South Shields

Sweet Land

I took a walk down to Sweet Land
What do I see?
Candyfloss clouds floating through the air
Very sticky lollipops as a tree
Popcorn river floating down the stream
Rainbow Drops falling from the sky
Candy cane lamp posts shining so brightly
Gingerbread people live in houses made of
chocolate
Jelly baby children with chocolate mice for pets
But, will you take a walk down to Sweet Land?

Ani Elizabeth Dowie (7)
Hadrian Primary School, South Shields

Topsy-Turvy World

A topsy-turvy world where all is not what it seems

The fish are in the sky
The birds are underwater
As topsy as topsy can be
The sharks are whistling happily
The submarine is blowing clouds everywhere
The birds blow bubbles underwater
I smell fish and chips floating above my hair
The octopus saying hello to the fish in the sky
As topsy-turvy as it could be.

Aisha Ansary (7)
Hadrian Primary School, South Shields

Magic Potion

I found a magical potion
Then, I drank it
When I got to the last drop
I saw something in the grass
When I looked around
I noticed I was a ladybird
There were birds rapping in the long, tall tree
There was a weird creature, it was a centipede
It was wearing a farmer's hat and little boots
I was sad to be so small
What if someone stands on me?

Kyra-Leigh Riley (8)
Hadrian Primary School, South Shields

Everything Changed

I went to school on a normal day
But suddenly, everything changed

The classroom is a planet
The teacher is an alien
Outside, there is an aeroplane with eyes
The children drank their cola
They fell fast asleep
The books were talking to the ruler
The felt tips were talking to the scissors

This place is too weird
I want to go home!

Hanifa Ahmed (8)
Hadrian Primary School, South Shields

Riding A Pony

I was flying on a magical pony across the sky
I looked around
There was a giraffe with purple spots flying by
There was the sun playing the loud trumpet
As I was flying by
I licked the clouds, it tasted like candyfloss
I heard the milkshake splashing
As it fell from the sky
Would you like a magical pony ride across the sky?

Kayan Uddin (8)
Hadrian Primary School, South Shields

My Friend Kite

I played with my friend, the kite
Kite was fast and crazy, it had lots of energy too
We had an argument and Kite ran off!
I flapped my arms and I flew off after Kite
I saw mermaids and dragons
I saw unicorns playing Tig
I saw Kite off in a huff
Screaming with rage
There he is!
That energetic friend of mine!

Amirah Zarrin Khazaeli (8)

Hadrian Primary School, South Shields

Sweet Land

I went to space on a table
Houses with windows that have eyes
But why?
I don't know
Children driving cars
Flying hamburgers
I am eating sweets from the sky
I don't know why, but I really love sweets
Invisible remote making people pause
I don't know why, but I am lost!

Hayyan Muhammad (7)
Hadrian Primary School, South Shields

Skating On A Rainbow

Skating on a rainbow, oh
What do you think I will see?

Cotton candy clouds
Chocolate fountain waterfall
Milky Way stars shining in the sky
Maltesers raining on my head
Sugar Strand Doughnuts float
Along the chocolate river

I want to stay here forever!

Lacey Bryden (7)
Hadrian Primary School, South Shields

A Weird Journey

My bath took me to a magical place
I saw dolphins riding bikes
I saw a giraffe, candy-like
I heard somebody singing
I smelled unicorn poop, yuck!
Sounds a bit weird, but this is Imagination Land
If you can, eat unicorn poop
That is very yucky
I want to live here!

Lily McLackland (8)
Hadrian Primary School, South Shields

Falling Cheese Rocks

The aliens were munching all the cheese rocks
Then, more cheese rocks came down, banging
When the cheese rocks came down and smashed
The cheese rocks never stopped coming down
The cheese on the rocks was very tasty and hot
Then, we ate some cheese rocks and had a picnic.

Eshaan Yusuf Mirza (7)
Hadrian Primary School, South Shields

Fish Planet

The fish is wet
The fish is a slippery, gold fish
Smells disgusting like rotten cheese
The fish is cold like ice
I could see 1,000 twinkling stars
The fish flew to a planet
They landed with a splash!
But there was no water to be seen.

James Thomas Robe (7)
Hadrian Primary School, South Shields

A Picnic With Animals

I went to a picnic with animals on a cloud
I heard a frog shouting out loud
I saw a rainbow flower made out of candyfloss
Ate dragons scales made out of moss
Me and my rabbit friend saw a dog
He jumped on a big, big log.

Saleema Ahad (7)
Hadrian Primary School, South Shields

Impulse Grenades Flying

I woke up to find myself in space
I saw a grey impulse grenade
I could hear weird alien noises from it
I wondered what it was for
I threw it on the ground
Then, I flew so high into the sky.

Yaseen Islam (8)
Hadrian Primary School, South Shields

SpongeBob Land

S quare pants

P ineapple house

O cean

N aughty Plankton

G ary the snail

E ugene

B urger

O ctopus

B ikini Bottom.

Arfath Chowdhury (8)

Hadrian Primary School, South Shields

Substitute Unicorn?

I was waiting for the teacher in class
And the time was really starting to pass
All of a sudden, a unicorn walked in
Everyone stared at it, open-mouthed
It said it was our substitute teacher, at last
As it passed me, its fluffy, rainbow tail
Swished in my face
It smelled of sweets and chocolate
Its hair was down to the floor
It was rainbow-coloured, obviously!
It was pink and fluffy
I just wanted to stroke it!

Suddenly, it stopped and had a poo!
It probably thought it was normal to go to the loo
But, the poo wasn't normal, it was more... colourful
Miss Unicorn went out of class, so I sneaked over
Wait... OMG! They were Smarties!
I felt like I'd found a four-leaf clover
I popped one in my mouth

It tasted heavenly.
Who knew poop could taste so fabulous?

Chloe Moore-Burgess (11)

Howard Junior School, Gaywood

A Cow And His Pet Toaster

There was a cow on the street
And it was eating all the sugar beet
He also had a pet toaster
But then, the cow
Made people go, "Ow!"
But the toaster
Was on a roller coaster
And then went back to the cow
Who was eating all the crows
And stole all the Cheddar cheese
And, after getting it all, he left
But, at least the toaster was good
And the food was really good as well
Then, it was time to ring the bell
As the cow was dead
But the toaster wasn't!

Alex Summers (10)
Howard Junior School, Gaywood

Dancing With Donald Trump

I asked Donald Trump to dance
I said to give it a chance

I was interested in what he did
I told him my name was Sid

I noticed his floppy hair
I didn't like to stare

Trump had a really good tan
But I just wasn't a fan

He seemed to have two left feet
That didn't move to the beat

He was always in the news
Wearing his size twelve shoes

The song came to an end
He said, "It was nice to meet you, my friend."

Evie Dye (10)
Howard Junior School, Gaywood

Did You Hear That Baby Dinosaur Sing?

"Did you hear? Did you hear,
that baby dinosaur sing?"
"No, no, no, what did it say?"
"It said that you are beautiful in every way."
The cheese unicorn neighed with pride,
"I hope that dinosaur didn't lie!"
"Hello, hello! I'm the dinosaur!
I sing about unicorns and
How beautiful they are."
"Well, thank you, thank you for the compliment
Now I'm going to fly away and become
A pink, fluffy car."

Ruby Davey (11)
Howard Junior School, Gaywood

Cereal Boxes Come To Life!

I'm walking to the cereal aisle in the shop
Everyone surrounding me
Staring at every step I take
I get to the cereal aisle and have a weird feeling
A box falls off the shelf
Little things start to creep out
I knew they were up to something without a doubt
Then, something comes off the box
I look closely to see it's a monkey
I chase it all around the shop
And end up bumping into the manager.

Alana McNeice (11)
Howard Junior School, Gaywood

The Basketball Game

My game of basketball didn't quite go to plan
The other team were 6ft flamingos
Not one was a man
It began to rain cabbages
Which wasn't much fun
The strawberry laces in my shoes
Kept coming undone
The ball was getting popped
By the unicorn's horn
The crowd just laughed
While eating popcorn
It was the strangest game I'd ever played
However, the memories would never fade.

Kirsty Allan (10)
Howard Junior School, Gaywood

Crazy Dream

In my dream last night
I dreamed about crazy things
I dreamed about talking ants
And they said, "I love your shirt!"
I dreamed about a man
With a balloon on his head
He was floating in the air

I dreamed about upside down buildings
Cars, people and a shark

I dreamed about people
Going into a cactus
And having a genie as a pet
That was the craziest dream ever!

Luke Murphy (10)
Howard Junior School, Gaywood

Feeling Magic!

I touch a chair and it starts walking
Things are weird around here
If normal objects grow duck legs
You have the magic touch!
Feeling magic, feeling magic
That tingly feeling in your finger

Objects moving and flying
There's definitely something
Weird going on here

Whatever you touch comes to life
Weird, walking walls and small, soft sofas
Coming to life unexpectedly.

Letysha Smith (11)
Howard Junior School, Gaywood

The Peculiar Orangutan!

After I went to bed
I heard a bang
I looked out the window
It was an orangutan!
It swung through the trees
Like they normally do
But this one was peculiar
Its fur was bright blue
I called my family
As we looked together
Instead of a tail
We saw a peacock feather!
It swung right past us
As we stared in awe
Soon, it was gone
To be seen no more!

Holly McDowell (11)
Howard Junior School, Gaywood

My Sister Turned Into A Parrot

My sister turned into a parrot
I couldn't believe my eyes
She had only eaten a carrot
Then, she flew up into the sky

Her skin had turned into feathers
Bright colours shone in the sun
All of the birds flew together
She had so much fun

I wanted to be a parrot
So I went into my kitchen
I ate a tiny piece of carrot
And only turned into a pigeon!

Preston Harrowing (10)
Howard Junior School, Gaywood

A Flying Donkey

I was sitting in my friend's bedroom
When, suddenly, there was a big boom!
I looked out the window
To see a glow
Which turned out to be a donkey!
Well, that surprised me!
He was flying in the sky
Up so high
Like a little butterfly
My, oh my.
What a sight to the eye
Well, that was the end of that
He fell to the ground with a splat!

Evie Lester (11)
Howard Junior School, Gaywood

The Random Dragon

I met a dragon today
He was the loveliest fellow
I was on his back
He was very black
He had red fire coming out of his mouth
I told him he had to sleep
I touched the clouds
They were very silky
Then, he started to roar
I said, "What's wrong?"
All he did was roar.
"Okay, it's alright," I said to him.

Derrick Bowditch (10)
Howard Junior School, Gaywood

On The Voyage Of Bewilderment

On the voyage of bewilderment, I made
A ballistic, balancing beaver
With the confidence of a lion

On the voyage of bewilderment, I made
A towering tarantula
Taught by the trees
And as thin as paper

On the voyage of bewilderment, I made
A whispering wolf like the whispering willow
Singing a lullaby

On the voyage of bewilderment, I made
An old, wise owl, as old and wise
As all the books in the library

On the voyage of bewilderment, I made
Eleven elegant elephants
Shimmering like moonlight.

Emily D (9)
Mendham Primary School, Mendham

In The Habitat Of Curiosity

In the Habitat of Curiosity, I created
Fantastic flying ferrets
Full of funniness like a comedian

In the Habitat of Curiosity, I created
Slippery snakes sliding through the sizzling snow
And fish feeling frantic, like a babysitter
With too many children to look after

In the Habitat of Curiosity, I created
A cheeky cheetah as speedy as
A strike of lightning

In the Habitat of Curiosity, I created
Pink pigs full of purple planes
Like a war museum
Full of planes from the war

In the Habitat of Curiosity, I created
A dog wearing a dazzling shirt and dusty shoes

Dancing on the mucky stairs
Dancing like a disco dancer.

Georgia Hearney (8)
Mendham Primary School, Mendham

In The Forest Of Fury

In the Forest of Fury, I made
1,000 flying ferrets as big as lions
And as fast as cheetahs

In the Forest of Fury, I made
A cat-eating kitten covered in cream
And as slow as a snail

In the Forest of Fury, I made
A million awesome antelopes
Always annoying ants

In the Forest of Fury, I made
A fantastic flying ferret full of fury
And the tail was shaped like a banana

In the Forest of Fury, I made
A furry, fantastic fox
As thin as a ruler.

Rishi French (8)
Mendham Primary School, Mendham

Trail Of Excitement

On the Trail of Excitement, I made
An excellent, excited elephant
That could fly like a hawk that parties

On the Trail of Excitement, I made
A wonderful, woolly mammoth
Like a dinosaur when angry

On the Trail of Excitement, I made
A perfect penguin that lived in the countryside

On the Trail of Excitement, I made
This grizzly bear that roars when hungry

On the Trail of Excitement, I made
A brilliant, blending blackbird
As big as a full stop.

Tess Walker (9)
Mendham Primary School, Mendham

Through The Forest Of Imagination

Through the Forest of Imagination, I made
A rampaging rabbit
Running as fast as a cheetah
With no respect

Through the Forest of Imagination, I made
A dancing dog in danger
And as fast as a dolphin

Through the Forest of Imagination, I made
A fighting fish as slow as a slug

Through the Forest of Imagination, I made
A random reindeer running as fast as rain

Through the Forest of Imagination, I made
A noisy narwhal as fast as a fish.

Emily (7)
Mendham Primary School, Mendham

Into The Forest Of Fun

In the Forest of Fun, I found
A kingdom of kiwi-eating kingfishers
As kind as a kitten

In the Forest of Fun, I found
A fairy rolling with flying fish
As fast as rolling cupcakes

In the Forest of Fun, I found
A load of lovely lemurs
Loading up with fruit of any kind

In the Forest of Fun, I found
A dabbing DJ dog
As dumb as a Dumbo

In the Forest of Fun, I found
A ferocious flying frog
Full of fury.

Aidan Layton Scott (9)
Mendham Primary School, Mendham

In The Forest Of Imagination

In the Forest of Imagination, I made
A cute kitten as fast as Usain Bolt

In the Forest of Imagination, I made
A flossing, frightening, fantastic ferret
As lazy as a snail

In the Forest of Imagination, I made
A flying, flossing fish
Like a bouncy kangaroo

In the Forest of Imagination, I made
A fat, fighting frog like a wolf

In the Forest of Imagination, I made
A bouncing bear as rapid as a cheetah.

Barney (7)
Mendham Primary School, Mendham

On The Island Of Magic

On the Island of Magic, I made
A snail slurp as speedily as a cheetah

On the Island of Magic, I made
A dangerous, diving dolphin
As strong as a killer whale

On the Island of Magic, I made
A ginormous giraffe
As tall as a lighthouse

On the Island of Magic, I made
A fantastic, floating, funny falcon
Flying through the air
As fast as a robin.

Luca Lambourn-Brown (8)
Mendham Primary School, Mendham

In The Forest Of Wonder

In the forest of wonder I made a weasel full of
wetness like a river.
In the forest of wonder I made a fantastic, flying,
fluffy ferret like a teddy bear.
In the forest of wonder I made a smiling, slow,
slithering snail-like goo.
In the forest of wonder I made a climbing silver cat
as gloomily as a suit.
In the forest of wonder I made a beautiful
bouncing butterfly like a kangaroo.

Harry Mattocks (7)
Mendham Primary School, Mendham

The Mountains Of Happiness

On the Mountains of Happiness, I saw
An elegant eagle ever so high

In the Forest of Wonder, I saw
A horse with a human head

In the sky of blue, I saw
A beautiful bird

On the journey of wonder, I made
An elegant elephant eating eggs
As fast as an elephant can

In the pool of see-through, I saw
A shark slithering.

Ellie Brown (8)
Mendham Primary School, Mendham

In The Forest Of Wonder

In the Forest of Wonder, I made
A sharp, hideous, pointed
And sharp Pikachu

In the Forest of Wonder, I made
A crazy snake with no confidence

In the Forest of Wonder, I made
A powerful, pointed pig
That had a lion's tail like Pikachu

In the Forest of Wonder, I made
A tickling tornado.

James (7)
Mendham Primary School, Mendham

On The Island Of Magic

On the Island of Magic, I made
A snail slurp as speedily as a cheetah runs

On the Island of Magic, I made
A dangerous dolphin
With teeth as sharp as
A killer whale's teeth

On the Island of Magic, I made
A giant, gargantuan giraffe
Taller than most houses.

Jackson R (7)
Mendham Primary School, Mendham

The Magic Box

Inspired by The Magic Box by Kit Wright

I will put in the box...
Silly snakes snow sledging
Laughing lions licking liquorice lollipops
Rotten Romans ruling Rome

I will put in the box...
Seven months in a year
Chocolate houses that never melt
Blue grass

I will put in the box...
A flat, square-shaped moon
Three solar systems
Cotton candy clouds

I will put in the box...
An eagle in the sea
A toad in the sky
A dolphin that walks
A human that swims in the sea
A ladybird jumping
A kangaroo flying

I will put in the box...
Building snowmen and snow walls
Whizzing down hills, sledging
Putting on woolly hats and scarves
Gloves, coats and earmuffs

I will put in the box...
A happy person going on holiday
A pretty poppy
A tall giant bouncing up and down

I will put in the box...
A fresh, clean cup of water
A cool, ice-cold ice cream
A bright and sparkly star

I will put in the box...
All of my family
My teddy bear called Teddy
And my pet hamster called Pebbles

My box is fashioned from
Diamonds and silver and emeralds
With hearts on the lid

And circles in the corners
Its hinges are pink and purple

In my box...
I will fly around the world
And see things I have never seen before
Then, I will teleport to different, unknown planets
And swim in a sea of chocolate

When I get back home
I will lie on my bed
The colour of a green emerald.

Lily Mersh (9)
Mill Hill Primary School, Sunderland

If I Were A Superhero

If I were a superhero
I would be able to fly
I'd wear a cape and fancy boots
And I would shoot through the sky

If I were a superhero
I would have special powers
I'd fly around and save the world
For hours and hours and hours

If I were a superhero
And you were in distress
I'd read your mind and see your thoughts
And save you from your stress

But I am not a superhero
I'm just a little girl
But, if you need me, I'll be there
I'll help you out, any time, anywhere.

Ava Mae Swinburne (8)

Mill Hill Primary School, Sunderland

Surfing On The Flaming Ends

Today is the day I'm going to be worried
I'm on a surfboard, cold but red
One slight movement and I'll be dead
My feet are swelling up
I've got a headache
My board's about to split
The lava's squirting up
The shiny galaxies are turning dull and grey
The bubbles are rising
The lava's spitting at me
My board is crumbling apart
My heart is beating very fast
While I'm watching the birds flutter by
Yelping and squawking at the volcano
In my bikini, my body is freezing
I keep on sneezing
Everybody is running away
While most of the children are out to play

The parents are screaming, "Get inside
Before the lava comes and burns your backside!"
So, the children are safe from the lava.

Toni Padgett (9)
Mill Hill Primary School, Sunderland

My Crazy Dream

I once had a dream
A few weeks ago
When I woke up
It was such a blow

It was about
Mermaids and sharks
And cats that liked
To bark

And, what they did
Don't let me start
Oh, if I must
I'll tell you a little part

The mermaids swam in soda
Eating candyfloss clouds
The sharks swam in chocolate milk
Not making a sound

The cat sat on chocolate
Eating gummy bears

He didn't look very busy
While licking his long, black hairs

Then, unfortunately, my alarm went off
And I felt the terrible truth
For now, it was time to go to school
With my sister, Ruth.

Grace Wheeler (9)
Mill Hill Primary School, Sunderland

A Little Wonderland

As the rainbow glistens in the afternoon sky
The pot of gold waits to be a prize

The leprechauns leap through fields of clover
Nudging, pushing, jumping over each other's
shoulders
How far will they run?
How far will they go?

The beautiful colours seem to go so far
Day turns to night, the moon begins
To shine bright
The leprechauns tire
And sit down to make a campfire

Maybe the prize will never be won
But the little wonderland will always be seen.

Eden-Lilly Isaacson (8)
Mill Hill Primary School, Sunderland

Candy Land

One morning, I woke up
I found out I was in a different land
It looked like it had lots of sweets
There were crunchy, caramel chocolate bars
There were also big, tall, giant lollipops
It was Candy Land!
I was so happy
I could not wait to go and eat a giant, large
lollipop
It was a strawberry-flavoured lolly
I also had some rainbow fizzy laces
They were yummy
I suddenly heard a beeping noise
I opened my eyes and saw it was all a dream
I loved Candy Land!

Chloe Duncton (8)
Mill Hill Primary School, Sunderland

If School Was A Nightmare

If school was a nightmare, here is how it would go
Hear the shouts, hear the cries
We get loads of homework
And always tell lies
We always tease, lose our bags
And bang our knees
We always share secrets
And tell jokes about old fellas and folks
The day doesn't go well
We wouldn't even tell if it was time to go home
And never come back
If you were a teacher, you would get the sack.

Sarah Grace Ivy Lovstad (9)
Mill Hill Primary School, Sunderland

I Tripped On A Rocket

I tripped on a rocket
I went flying in the sky
I saw all the people walking by
I saw Justin and Tom walking about
I did try to shout
But I was high in the sky
I waved goodbye
To the whole world
Then, I flew to a planet
Not sure of the name
But then, I saw a little, green man
But it was too late
I was not above like a dove
I was down below, back home.

Maisie Wilson (8)

Mill Hill Primary School, Sunderland

My Meatball Space Land

All up in space was a wacky adventure
With meatball asteroids flying through Mars
Skip on a rocket
Fry cheesy moon rocks
Run wild in space
As you blow bubbles into moon craters
Sit in a balloon and float
Instead, how about a ride in a pelican
In the sky for a very long time and high up
Feeling fire burn around my face
Watching rockets fly above space.

Oscar Drew (8)
Mill Hill Primary School, Sunderland

Mmm, Surprising Volcano

Bang!
I looked outside my window and, what a sight!
I saw a rumbling volcano that gave me a fright
It had exploded into the air
M&Ms were everywhere
This was strange to see
I saw a chocolate river heading towards me
Now, our home town
Is chocolatey brown
This is my town, you can see
There are M&Ms for you and me.

Raef Clegg-Cawood (9)
Mill Hill Primary School, Sunderland

Cookie World

I'm a mysterious monster living in a cookie world
With my pals: Dumb Dinosaur
And Dangerous Dragon

Cookie by day,
Cookie by night,
Watch out for Dangerous Dragon,
He'll sure give you a fright.

Cookie by day,
Cookie by night,
Watch out for Dumb Dinosaur,
He might give you a bite.

Heidi Pantall (9)
Mill Hill Primary School, Sunderland

Halloween

Bring a candle
Bring a light
It must be Halloween tonight

I saw a pixie
Small and fine
Dancing on the washing line

I saw a giant
Ten feet wide
With half a dozen ships inside

I saw a fairy
Like a dream
On top of the milk and sipping ice cream.

Chloe Hill (9)
Mill Hill Primary School, Sunderland

My Crazy Life

Computer games and football are the things I like
Especially FIFA and riding my bike
I like my clothes, my favourite brand is Nike
I also like being a school counsellor
I think about it every night
My name is Warren Edwards
And that was a brief poem about my crazy life.

Warren Dean Edwards (8)
Mill Hill Primary School, Sunderland

The Dance Of The Teacups

Teacups floating out of the door
Teacups on the floor

Teacups all together
Teacups forever

Teacups left and right
Teacups floating all night.

Megan O'Brien (9)
Mill Hill Primary School, Sunderland

Sweet-Mania

There is a planet in space that is far, far away
To go there means travelling
For more than one day
The planet is called Sweet-Mania
Everything on it is made of sugar and sweets
But be careful you don't over-eat

It has bouncy clouds of bubblegum
Everything on it tastes yum, yum
Where is this place, please tell me where
It has liquorice roads with lollipop lights
Carpets of chocolate and honeycomb bites

It has Toblerone mountains high in the sky
Gingerbread houses you don't need to buy
Where is this place, please tell me where
It has Smarties all over like grains of sand
This place is amazing, the best in the land.

Lexi Tindsley (10)
Northfield St Nicholas Primary School, Lowestoft

My Stinky Socks!

My stinky socks
Carry my rocks
Sometimes, my socks even jump around
And make my room stink up
My stinky socks
Give me chicken pox.

My smelly socks
Give me electric shocks
I run up and down
Until it finally stops
My smelly socks
Look like Goldilocks.

I'm sick and tired of these socks
Because they even broke my clocks
I hate them so much, but they're my socks
And I love my stinky socks
Lots and lots and lots.

Kaitlin Grace Cadence Collis (9)
Northfield St Nicholas Primary School, Lowestoft

The Flying Unicorn

A unicorn with a sparkly horn
And wings as fluffy as snow
Up, up and away it goes
Where to? Nobody knows
Its rainbow mane shimmers in the light
Her eyes sparkle like diamonds in the night
She lives in a wonderland of clouds
Sweets and glitter dust
It's the most magical place
Visiting there is a must!

Evie Armitage (7)
Northfield St Nicholas Primary School, Lowestoft

Candy Dream Life

There was a young girl from school
Who was sad because she'd dreamt of eating gruel
She woke up and was happy
As she was surrounded by candy
And she ate and she ate until she was full.

Megan-Jane Davey (8)
Northfield St Nicholas Primary School, Lowestoft

Pull A Pig's Tail

Pull a pig's tail
A merry story, I ought to tell
Once at night, a pig was sitting on the floor
In stones of hail
I said, "Poor pig, shall I bring you inside?"
He said, "Oh yes, it's cold out here!"
"Shall I feed you anything?"
"Oh yes! pizza and a couple of pink drinks would
be nice."
I fed him the pizza and the pink drinks
then, he asked me what the stars meant,
I reluctantly got up and took him outside
for he darest not hide.
We lay down and look at the lit up sky,
"Each of these stars have a special meaning,
now do you know what the stars mean?"
"Yes, I do!" cried the pig
"Yo oh he, pull my tail."
I gasped as the tail sprang in joy just like me!

Mia Iman Akinola (10)
Salisbury Primary School, Manor Park

My Clumsy Morning

When I first get up, I never want to open my eyes
But slowly, slowly, I think I might cry
Because I have to put my warm feet
On the cold, cold floor
Which does not look very warm
I go down from my room to the living room
Where I spot yummy pancakes
The first bite tastes like heaven
Yummy, yummy in my tummy
I think I might like some more
But sadly, there's no time
Because it's time for school
So I get ready in my soft, cosy clothes
I brush my teeth, Mom shouts
"Time is ticking!"
In a rush, we're at school.

Simrah Rahman (9)
Salisbury Primary School, Manor Park

Clear, With A Chance Of Moons!

T'was a clear night
With tiny specks of colourful stars
Some with chocolate chip cookie planets
And some with hamburger moons

One was brighter and bigger
With white and black craters
It was the moon
While the morning was breaking
Eventually, the moon disappeared

The earthlings went wild
The whistling of the elephants
The crowing of the pigs
The screaming of the cows
The oinking of the horses
The neighing of the humans

After a lot of wickedness
The white, spherical thief appeared again
Almost at the same time, they stopped

It was night
Clear, with a chance of moons!

Shaurya Umesh (9)
Salisbury Primary School, Manor Park

Mother

My life with you is the peace in my heart
My life without you is the darkness of my life
You and only you are there
When the sunlight goes away
Or the moon disappears
Mother, you are the hope to my dream
And the key to my success
You are the sunshine to my soul
But also sometimes the poison to my veins
The poison to my veins that's what some people say
But you are truly the person I live for
There are many ups and downs
But our love never disappears
Leaving your life, you create mine
Leave your fantasy, you create mine.

Shaeba Hossain (9)
Salisbury Primary School, Manor Park

My Genie

My genie is so cool
He doesn't go to school
He lounges all day
And chills by his pool

Anytime I want a wish
The lamp I have to itch
He comes out in a jiffy
And looks all smart and pretty

My wish is his command
I can make three wishes a day
I can ask for anything I want
And he has to do what I say

A funny fact about my genie
His name is Robin, but I call him Tony
I gave him this nickname because
He likes macaroni.

Hamza Abad (9)
Salisbury Primary School, Manor Park

Valentine

Violets are beautiful, just like you
Anyone can be a star,
But you are the brightest of them all
Laughter I like to share with you
Every day is a fun one with you
Not every friend is as fun as you
Time with you is time well spent
I think you are a friend in a million
Not everyone is as special as you
Every day, I look forward to seeing you
Special days are made for you.

Elizabeth-Rose Kelly (9)
Salisbury Primary School, Manor Park

My Underground World

U nder the ground, where spirits lay
N o one has ever been here but me
D oves bounce around, singing sweetly
E lves are my servants, as sweet as pie
R abbits love flying, it's so much fun
G round squirrels love the sweet smells
R ound caramel fountain
O verhead candyfloss bridge
U nder the bridge are perfume lilies
N ow, there is a gummy castle as sweet as perfume
D own in the dungeons of despair, it is slimy

W e live in peace and happiness
O ur world is kind and gentle
R eeds around perfume lilies
L ovely gummy bear rides
D own in my secret lair, I can always hide.

Islay de Gonville Bromhead (7)

South Lee School, Bury St Edmunds

Gummy Bears

G ummy bears, yummy, gummy, gummy, gummy bears!

U se just more of the ingredients to make the big ones

M y gummy bears are so small

M agic bears, magic bears, yummy magic bears

Y ummy, yummy, yummy bears

B ut I do not like them small

E xciting times are when the packets get bigger!

A nd there you are, a giant one!

R eady, get set, go! Yum yum yum!

S o gummy bears? Giant gummy bears that are great!

Charlotte Grigg (7)

South Lee School, Bury St Edmunds

It With A Mouse

I would love to play It with a mouse
There are so many places to hide in my house
Under the sink, through the hole
I wonder what it is like under that coat?
Quiet as mice, counting to ten
I wonder if he will find me in my den?
Tiny gaps through the floorboards
Better not mess up the piano chords
Playing It with a mouse would be fun
Although I think it would always be the mouse that
won.

Daisy Katherine Martineau (7)
South Lee School, Bury St Edmunds

Sweety World

I went to this world that was not like the others
I ate some sweets to fill my tummy
I saw a clown that was funny
Everything was so yummy
Scrumptious, sweet, sour and sticky
This could all get a bit tricky
Sugar and spice and all things nice
Flying saucers, Drumsticks and Squashies
This world is making me happy!

Darcey O'Farrell (7)
South Lee School, Bury St Edmunds

Raining Chocolate Drops

Imagine if, instead of water
We had chocolate for rain!
No more moaning and everyone
Would be excited for the rain
Children would jump in choccy puddles
And we'd all walk around
With our mouths open
And Mummy would shout
"Don't tread chocolate into the house!"

Amélie Grace Swanton (7)
South Lee School, Bury St Edmunds

The Magic Pipe

Everything I check on a pipe
It starts to creak and leak
I creep inside and, what do I see?
A magic world, wow!
The door only opens for me
I have a tea party
The huge factory is where it all starts
Candy snowing from the chimney
I am so happy I fell asleep!

Alev Warwick (8)
South Lee School, Bury St Edmunds

Dream World

Jumping on a cloud
Grabbing some marshmallows
I watched a dragon fly through the sky
Why not grab some candyfloss
Watching a Jelly Baby with no legs
And burgers bobbing below
I see a baby dragon hatch.

Sophie Johnson (7)
South Lee School, Bury St Edmunds

My Land Of Party

The sun is shining
Sweets are dancing with joy
Here, love and joy never end
Toffee fountain never stops
Trees are never sweeter
Smelling their perfume
The party never stops!

Elli O'Dwyer (8)
South Lee School, Bury St Edmunds

Imagination Wonderland

In my dreams, I could see
A world waiting up for me
It's full of possibilities

There's a mushroom that bubbles
It looked like it might cause trouble
I felt it and it was like rubble

I met a tree
My fortune, it told me
It had a golden key

Standing by the river was a teacup
It asked me if we could meet up
I said, "Of course you little flea cup."

I have to go, it's morning now
So I'll see you tomorrow
My little Imagination Wonderland!

Beth Patterson (9)
Stalham Academy, Stalham

My Unicorn Clown!

Four-legged tightrope
Unicycle mad
Beep! Beep!
Honk! Honk!
Nothing could be bad!

Magical castle kingdom
Flying everywhere
As long as I'm with you, I just don't care!
Fur as soft as an angel
Trotting along with me
I think you're as graceful as a great queen bee

You're my unicorn clown
And I like it that way
I love you for who you are
Celebrating your birthday
All through the day!

Phoebe Laws (9)
Stalham Academy, Stalham

Springtime

Daisies and dandelions, trees and bees
And flowers that are as pretty as can be
Springtime is found, no wonder why it came
Because winter is wintry and cold
That's why springtime comes
Spring is beautiful like your heart
Your heart is graceful and kind
Bees are beautifully dancing
Birds are swooping like magic in the sky
Flowers are shooting out as fairy wands
Spring, spring, spring, springtime is for everyone.

Olivia Ford (8)
Stalham Academy, Stalham

I Love Candyland

I would love to go to Candyland
It's probably a wonderland
But, will there be UFOs
Or bows and arrows?

I would love to go to Candyland
There's probably candy sand
But, will there be talking gummy bears
Can I bring my teddy bears?

I would love to go to Candyland
With all of this
But, it doesn't matter
Because I live in Candyland!

Kaitlin Collins (10)
Stalham Academy, Stalham

Roaming Romans

The reign of the roaming Romans
A tragic time
Full of disaster and death
Rome and Romans
Are all that is left
The reign of the roaming Romans
And roaming through the land
Conquering London and other lands
Through cities and forests
Waiting for a battle full of their last breaths
Never before a survivor left
Trying their best for good.

Zebedee Mixer (9)
Stalham Academy, Stalham

My Special Unicorn

I once flew on a rainbow unicorn
We flew high into the sky
He loved to eat popcorn
This is what made him fly
We took off like a rocket to a faraway land
The best way to fly, I rode him with one hand
The path was bright and beautiful
It sparkled, shimmered and shone
The most wonderful sight you have ever seen
Shooting rainbows from his behind.

Phoebe Sue Dorrington (7)
Stalham Academy, Stalham

How I Feel

I lie awake
Night after night
Not even with myself
Can I put up a fight

I have no idea
But it will never show
People ask me how I am
But I will never know

People are happy
I am sad
They say about the good
I think about the bad

Life is different
Life is changing
Life is just now for the taking.

Amy Frisby (11)
Stalham Academy, Stalham

Labrador

L ovely creatures that are cute
A mazing animals
B eloved family pet
R acing around the garden
A dorable, fluffy dog
D aring, digging, dirty dog
O utgoing, fun, loving canines
R eally good friend.

Ben Townshend (7)
Stalham Academy, Stalham

The Undertaking Experience Of The Badger And The Squid

There once was a badger and a squid
The badger could swim underwater, he was a kid
The squid used to rest and the badger would try
and scare the little guy.

But the squid was not happy and found
That he had eyes in the back of his head
He used to sit and watch
As swift as a butterscotch

And the badger would swim down
And he would frown
Because the squid attacked him 'til he was dead
Then, the squid fled

The squid gave one last shout
As he looked at the last piece of the badger -
Its snout.

Tegan Barrett (11)
Tregadillett Primary School, Tregadillett

The Snow, The Desert And The Rocket

Something went awry with my rocket launch

It was mild, very mild, but snowy
So, the rocket froze over
I was expecting this to go wrong
I'd have to find a lucky clover
My magic ice cream melted
And the junk I built the rocket with
Was from my tumble dryer
I wish I had known that before
Because it stopped working years ago
I am a useless fairy, the lowest of the low
But, even then I realised that the engine would not go
But, finally, we launched it into space!
With me and Zion
Zion is my best friend
He stayed with me throughout

My name is Elspeth and I thought you'd like to know
My moon cheese was put behind bulletproof glass
And that glass was made of snow!

Ebony Seedell (9)

Tregadillett Primary School, Tregadillett

Andy And Mandy

There once was a fairy called Andy
And a unicorn called Mandy
Who both needed to survive on candy

They used to ignore
They both became weak and insecure
And ended up going to war

The unicorn, Mandy
Ate the fairy called Andy
And enjoyed all the candy

Andy came back and haunted Mandy
She stole all the candy
Which was very handy

And it taught Mandy a lesson
Don't pick on smaller animals.

Ava-Grace Phoebe Barrett (9)
Tregadillett Primary School, Tregadillett

Wonderland Madness

The rabbit, it talks
And the cat, it teleports
Mice, rats, cows
Kitties and owls

The clocks, they turn
And the balls, they roll
Careful where you stop
You might run into a troll

The trees all jump
And the leaves all wave
As the plants lead it's victim
Into the cave

The path winds
And the clouds rain
As the chocolate milk falls
You become a candy cane.

Leah Trewin (11)
Tregadillett Primary School, Tregadillett

A Wand In A Pond

There was once a wand in a pond
It sat there all day
People didn't really care about it
So they first walked away
I guess most people just sit in a pool
Getting cool
And I bet people wouldn't get hot
Because most people do not
They were never picked up
So bad luck
The wand wasn't found ever
Literally, it wasn't found, never
One day, someone found the wand
While it was in its baby blue pond
But, someone else wanted to pick it up
So he was very mad
And also very sad
Everyone clapped
And everyone rapped.

Freya Mepham-Gilbert (7)
Uplands Primary School, Sandhurst

Wonderful Magical World

It was the night before the magic began
All were silent, all were asleep
When one little girl
Peeked out of the dark
Out of the door and into the day
She found out everything was candy
She tasted the air and the clouds
They were very sweet
She tasted the sun and it was fun
She had never tasted anything like this
And said, "Night, night Sweet Land."
And went back to bed.

Payton Rae De Villiers (8)
Uplands Primary School, Sandhurst

There's A Slug In My Mug

There was a slug in my mug
But I took a big glug
I felt the slug
And put down my mug
I looked in my mug
And found the slug
I took out the slug
And drank from my mug
The slug tapped my shoulder
And gave me a boulder
I put him on my shoulder
And we sat on the boulder
We talked and talked
Until we grew older
And, when we said goodbye
We ate pumpkin pie.

Mariam Jabang (7)
Uplands Primary School, Sandhurst

The Beauty Of A Forest

I decide to go for a walk in the forest
While the sun is shining during a long August
As I elegantly skip through
I have a feeling like a detective, looking for a clue
There are bees buzzing by
And a sound of a baby bird's cry
Then, I walk into an old barn
To find hay, straw and a bit of old yarn
As I walk further and faster
I feel like I've travelled to the past
As I look out into a field that is clear
Then, there is a herd of big deer
I keep to the path covered in rocks
I see black and white sheep in their flocks
I keep walking on and it looks like a jungle
I see leaves, berries and ivy in a bundle
As I get to a road
I put myself in safety mode
When I get to my home
I suddenly feel all alone.

Ruby Violet Follen (10)
Weeting (VC) Primary School, Weeting

Palace Problems

The king had a loving daughter
They made their servants collect their water
The princess had a beautiful carriage
But, all it did was sit in the garage
The princess thought of crazy designs
Not to fit people with the right minds
The king was not a fashion stylist
So her designs would never be a miss
One day, the princess started a fashion store
Her designs would leave you never wanting more
So the princess grew distraught
But she could never be taught
The princess would never figure out fashion wasn't
her thing
But the poor king, she'd thought of a new hobby
She thought she'd learn how to sing.

Eloise Grass (9)
Weeting (VC) Primary School, Weeting

The Light Night

It's the one night of the year
When the moon doesn't appear
The sun takes its place
On the night's face
The foxes wake
Then, they quake
The owls do not know
Why the moon would go
The moon has gone on holiday
To somewhere far away
Eating a snack
He said, "Soon I will be back."
Later, he played bingo
And said, "Yo!"
Back in the wood
The animals thought this could
Yes, it could and should be over
Oh wait, it's the day
Next year is not far away
Look, the moon is back
And it's all normal.

Dorothy Childerhouse (9)

Weeting (VC) Primary School, Weeting

An Elf Sleepover!

I invited a friend to tea
When he arrived, I wasn't that pleased
It was an elf far from myself
He had a baby dragon
Which he carried around in a wagon
He told me he was curious
Of what we humans do
I said to him, "You are... who?"
He looked at me as if I was rude
And happily ate my stew
I said, "Should we be friends?"
He pleaded with joy and sang so loud
So now I can no longer hear a sound
So now, every week
The elf comes to me
And, as you can imagine
My mum's not that pleased.

Sienna Lilly Lexi White (10)
Weeting (VC) Primary School, Weeting

What I Saw This Morning

I saw a girl this morning
Whilst everyone was snoring
She laughed then screamed
As her huge smile beamed
She had this thing I'd never seen before
And it was so fascinating
It was certainly no bore
The next morning came
So I went to the window to find her again
Have you seen anything like this before?
I've seen it once and want more and more!
It's such a nice feeling when I see that girl
It must be magic or is it a pearl..?

Ellie Doll Ellis (8)

Weeting (VC) Primary School, Weeting

Autumn

The leaves are red
Pumpkins are orange
And the moon is bright
Everyone looks up in fright
Jack-o'-lanterns light up the night
Decorations are put up to scare
Ghosts and goblins, beware!

Sophia Rose Harrison (9)
Weeting (VC) Primary School, Weeting

Me And My Unibunny!

Unibunny eating a candy cane
What has the world come to?
I'll tell you
It's coming to Unibunny Land!

If I were in Brazil
My Unibunny would catch a chill
Poor, poor Bill the Unibunny

If I were in Spain
My Unibunny would eat a candy cane

If I were in Water World
My Unibunny would shout and scream

If I were the Queen of Hearts
My Unibunny would shout and dance.

Lou Lou Rolfe (9)
Woodbridge Primary School, Woodbridge

Zombie Attack!

With one blink of an eye
I was a lightling!
I was so strong like a gong
Then, a zombie cookie came at me

Then, a war started
I was the best one of them all!

I don't know how
But Frankie the Bengal came
With his sidekick, Mr Lego Brick
I would also have a bullet ant on my team.

Andrew Hunter Huisman (9)
Woodbridge Primary School, Woodbridge

Mad Rabid Seal!

Mad Rabid Seal loves to have tea
But Mad Rabid Seal's friends don't agree

Mad Rabid Seal also loves pie
When he runs out of it, he starts to cry

Mad Rabid Seal is crazy
So he picks a rainbow daisy

Mad Rabid Seal loves to have fun
He thinks fun is for everyone!

Cate Hesketh (8)
Woodbridge Primary School, Woodbridge

Teddy Poem

Walking teddy bears walking down the hall
Dancing and prancing to the lolly pool
They got to the pool and said goodbye
To their old pal Mikeymi
They cheered hooray for the man who saved the
day
Teddy's dog was as big as a frog
And there were talking lollipops cleaning with
mops.

Matilda Wade (9)

Woodbridge Primary School, Woodbridge

The Animal Journey

There was a dog
She danced and pranced
She was even from France

There was a monkey
He was chunky
He was cool and funky

Cats are big, cats are small
Some are good, some are not at all
Some wear top hats, sit on gnats
Some sit on mats.

Maggie Vinton (8)
Woodbridge Primary School, Woodbridge

YOUNG WRITERS INFORMATION

We hope you have enjoyed reading this book – and that you will continue to in the coming years.

If you're a young writer who enjoys reading and creative writing, or the parent of an enthusiastic poet or story writer, do visit our website **www.youngwriters.co.uk**. Here you will find free competitions, workshops and games, as well as recommended reads, a poetry glossary and our blog. There's lots to keep budding writers motivated to write!

If you would like to order further copies of this book, or any of our other titles, then please give us a call or visit **www.youngwriters.co.uk**.

Young Writers
Remus House
Coltsfoot Drive
Peterborough
PE2 9BF
(01733) 890066
info@youngwriters.co.uk

Join in the conversation!
Tips, news, giveaways and much more!

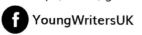 YoungWritersUK  @YoungWritersCW